powers, while exploiting his radicalism to threaten e: the event of a major confrontation over the nuclear issue.

* President Ahmadinezhad seems to have accepted that Khamenei defines the overall framework of Iranian policy and the president implements the policies and strategies. However, the crux of the matter is that Khamenei and Ahmadinezhad have different assessments of the risks that the regime will have to take in pursuit of its nuclear programme and regional strategies. It is highly unlikely that the issue will be completely resolved in the near to medium term because the issue is closely intertwined with leadership and factional politics in Iran.

Contents

Iranian Strategy: Factionalism & Leadership Politics

Dr Babak Ganji

Ahmadinezhad's domestic base:
the alliance with Ayatollah Mesbah-Yazdi

The Iranian presidential elections of 2005 led to a realignment of forces in Iran's clerical establishment. Perhaps the most notable change was the emergence of a political alliance between the radical supporters of Iranian President Mahmud Ahmadinezhad and the ultra-conservative Hojjatieh Society, whose members were castigated as representatives of "American Islam" in the 1980s. Another major realignment was the formation of a de facto alliance between the reformists and the right-of-centre Executives of Construction Party which supports former president and head of the Expediency Council Akbar Hashemi-Rafsanjani. The alliance between the reformists and Rafsanjani during the presidential elections split conservative clerics in Iran. Although most conservative clerics tacitly favoured Rafsanjani in 2005, the alliance between Ahmadinezhad's Islamic Developers Coalition and the conservative Islamic Coalition Society meant that initially the government was also supported by some prominent conservative clerics.

The political philosophy of both the Islamic Developers Coalition and Islamic Coalition Society is based on the assumption that the supreme leader receives his authority from God and is therefore above criticism. Ayatollah Ali Khamenei has himself indicated that he is above the law and that he receives his authority from God. He has said that the Islamic Republic was not "prepared to allow flawed and non-divine perspectives and ideas that are aimed at enhancing the power of the individual to dictate its social and political lives".[1] This position is essentially diametrically opposed to that of the reformists, who have repeatedly stressed the importance of republicanism in Khomeyni's teachings.

Since the 2005 presidential elections republicanism has been the only unifying theme for a wide array of reformist, right of centre and left-of-centre political groups in the country. On the whole, within the establishment the strongly pro-Khatami Islamic Iran Participation Front and the Islamic Revolution Mojahedin Organization are most in favour of emphasizing the republican character of the Iranian state. At the level of civil society, the so-called "national-religious" groups such as the Iran Freedom Movement have been stressing the importance of republicanism.

Rafsanjani's alliance with the reformists meant that the republican agenda was being represented even in such elite institutions as the Expediency Council and the Assembly of Experts, thereby raising questions about the longevity of Khamenei's rule. That was the main reason why Khamenei has been supporting the alliance between Ahmadinezhad's Islamic Developers Coalition and the Islamic Coalition Party, which has been a bastion of traditional religious conservatism in Iran since long before the fall of the Shah, and in that respect provided much needed ideological legitimacy to Khamenei's rule.

1

However, the alliance between Ahmadinezhad and the Islamic Coalition Party has been fractured by a number of serious disputes, ranging from nuclear to economic policy. This has also led Ayatollah Khamene'i to seek to broaden his own power base lest the president's declining popularity and radicalism lead to a direct attack on his own position.[2]

During the elections, Ahmadinezhad made efforts to portray himself as a pious politician and repeatedly invoked his commitment to Islamism and justice to challenge his rival Rafsanjani, who was considered to be one of the most corrupt politicians in the country. After the elections, Ahmadinezhad made a point of travelling to the city of Qom to meet senior clerics. Reportedly, a number of them refused to meet him. He responded by appointing the former commander of the navy, Admiral Mohtaj, as the governor-general of the province. There was a crackdown on Sufis and a growing rift between the government and the clergy.[3]

After the elections, Ayatollah Muhammad Taqi Mesbah-Yazdi's name surfaced as a possible successor to Ayatollah Khamenei, despite his having been criticized for his lack of revolutionary credentials.[4] However, Mesbah-Yazdi was among those members of the Assembly of Experts who could be relied upon to side with Khamene'i in the event of a confrontation with former president Khatami over the course of the reform programme. In contrast, Khamene'i's strongest supporters among senior clerics, ayatollahs Fazel-Lankarani, Behjat and Nuri-Hamedani, lack political credentials or any networks of political supporters.

Efforts to buttress Khamene'i's position should also be assessed within the context of the radicals' attempt to co-opt the Hojjatieh Society. Hojjatieh was an anti-Baha'i semi-secret society formed in the 1950s. During the Iranian revolution, it did not support the establishment of the rule of the supreme jurisconsult which was the centrepiece of Ayatollah Khomeyni's teachings. Instead, members of Hojjatieh favoured collective religious leadership and opposed religious involvement in politics. After the revolution, however, the founder of Hojjatieh, Sheikh Mahmud Halabi, who was concerned about a communist victory in Iran, called on his followers to abandon their ideas and support the establishment of an Islamist government. Hojjatieh dissolved itself in 1983 when Khomeyni called on it to "get rid of factionalism and join the wave that is carrying the nation forward".[5]

A powerful member of Hojjatieh after the revolution, Ayatollah Mohammad Hoseyni-Beheshti, was involved in setting up Haqqani Theological Seminary which has been instrumental in training senior Iranian intelligence and Judiciary officials.[6] Ayatollah Mesbah-Yazdi was also a founder of the seminary and lectures there.[7] The advent of the Ahmadinezhad government led prominent Iranian political figures, primarily supporters of former President Mohammad Khatami, to warn of the re-emergence of Hojjatieh. There were two Haqqani alumni in the Ahmadinezhad cabinet, Intelligence Minister Hojjat ol-Eslam Gholamhoseyn Mohseni-Ezhe'i and Interior Minister Mostafa Purmohammadi.[8] Shortly after President Ahmadinezhad's inauguration, former President Khatami warned that an extremist movement had emerged which was trying instil fears of corruption and warning that university curricula were not sufficiently Islamic.[9] Such fears of were stoked by the activities of Ayatollah Mesbah-Yazdi. For example, in July 2005 he claimed that the 12th Shi'i Imam had prayed for Ahmadinezhad's election.

President Ahmadinezhad's references to the 12th Imam in his speech at the UN in September 2005 and his later claim that he felt surrounded by an aura during his speech which also captivated the audience led to sharp criticisms of his behaviour. There were reports that Ahmadinezhad had allocated millions of dollars from the public treasury for the Jamkaran mosque in the suburbs of Qom where some believe the Hidden Imam will reappear.[10] Ahmadinezhad's supporters among the clergy have been sharply criticized and accused of demagoguery. For example, a reformist member of parliament, Emad Afruq, accused "pseudo-clerics" of promoting "mysticism", "distorting Islam" and "misleading the faithful".[11]

There have been reports by Iranian émigrés and some conservative American authors that Mesbah-Yazdi has emerged as a rival of Ayatollah Ali Khamene'i.[12] On this view, Ahmadinezhad's references to the 12th Imam are aimed at sidelining Khamenei and divesting the supreme leader of his political and administrative powers. Some of the proponents of this thesis have gone so far as to argue that in the event of a confrontation between Khamene'i and Mesbah-Yazdi, Khamene'i will side with clerics such as Rafsanjani to prevent Ahmadinezhad and Mesbah-Yazdi from taking over the Assembly of Experts, the leadership body which is responsible for "electing" Iran's supreme leader.[13]

However, there is no evidence other than hearsay and rumours to substantiate such claims. If anything, Mesbah-Yazdi has emerged as Khamene'i's key defender and repeatedly argued that the supreme leader is above criticism. Indeed, he offered Khamene'i support at a time when Khamene'i's opponents were trying to form a grand coalition to oppose him. In the 1990s, Mesbah-Yazdi emerged as one of the main advocates of violence to suppress the reform movement. He was named as one of a small group of clerics who issued fatwas justifying the assassination of dissidents.[14] Mesbah-Yazdi has argued that republicanism is not as important as the guardianship of the supreme jurisconsult and has suggested that the supreme jurisconsult does not have to allow the people to elect their own president.

During the 2005 presidential elections, two candidates, Mostafa Mo'in and former President Rafsanjani raised the issue of modifying the constitution to curtail the powers of the supreme jurisconsult.[15] Since the elections, the Ahmadinezhad government has taken a number of steps to ensure that the jurisconsult would not be attacked by his political opponents. They include: (a) suspension of the constitutional supervisory board set up by former President Khatami; (b) calling for the prosecution of those guilty of perpetrating "economic crimes", a thinly veiled reference to Rafsanjani; (c) preventing former Majlis Speaker Mehdi Karrubi from setting up a satellite TV network. At the same time, Minister of Culture and Islamic Guidance Hoseyn Saffar-Harandi, a prominent radical and ally of Ayatollah Mesbah-Yazdi, has been taking draconian measures against reformist and dissident journalists and publications. The reformists have come to the conclusion that they will have to directly attack Khamene'i's position to bring about a change of strategy.

Ahmadinezhad's domestic difficulties and nuclear policy

A continuing challenge from Rafsanjani and his close ally, former secretary of the Supreme National Security Council and chief nuclear negotiator, Hasan Rowhani did not stop Ahmadinezhad from pressing forward with his policies. He sought to galvanize support at the popular level for purging his opponents although he refused to name them publicly. At the same time, Ahmadinezhad continued to call into question the Holocaust and sought to build regional support for a policy of focussing attention on Israel. It is important to note that the president's denial of the Holocaust had little to do with his domestic difficulties. The Holocaust has never been a key issue in domestic Iranian politics. The domestic aspects of the power struggle were dealt with through the president's anti-corruption campaign, which was organized around the theme of fighting profiteering and nepotism. The policy of Holocaust denial, which was strongly supported by Khamene'i and the

3

Islamic Revolutionary Guards Corps, was aimed at derailing efforts by the fledgling coalition between a variety of reformist groups and Rafsanjani's Executives of Construction Party to revert Iran's regional strategy, and by extension its nuclear policy, to selective cooperation with the US on Iraq and Afghanistan, and to persuade the US to make concessions to Iran on the nuclear issue.[16] Neither Khamene'i nor Ahmadinezhad believed that the US would stop at anything short of regime change. They assumed that their opponents' strategy would lead to a significant modification of the regime and their own removal from power.

Proponents of the theory of Khamene'i-Mesbah-Yazdi split argue that Ahmadinezhad has formed an alliance with Mesbah-Yazdi to challenge the supreme leader and the old clerical establishment.[17] There is hardly any evidence in support of this contention. The available evidence suggests that Ahmadinezhad's radical supporters in the Islamic Revolution Guards Corps and the clerical establishment are using Mesbah-Yazdi to persuade Khamene'i to change Iran's nuclear policy from bomb in the basement to weaponization in return for full political support. Ahmadinezhad's supporters seem to be using Mesbah-Yazdi to make a deal with Khamene'i; in return for mobilizing clerical support for Khamene'i, they want the weaponization option to be put on the table and possibly pursued due to the emerging US and Israeli threats to the regime.

Ayatollah Mesbah-Yazdi's former pupil, Hojjat ol-Eslam Mohsen Gharavian, has emerged as the unofficial spokesman of a group within the clerical establishment that favours nuclear opacity and has declared that the resort to nuclear warfare might be religiously permissible for defensive purposes.[18] This was a milestone in Iran's declaratory policy. Ayatollah Khamene'i has declared in a 'fatwa' or decree that nuclear weapons are "un-Islamic".[19] The evidence suggests that there was a major change in Khamene'i's position on the nuclear issue in February 2006. However, Khamenei did not himself articulate the change of policy.

During this period, Mohsen Gharavian, a pupil of Ayatollah Mesbah-Yazdi, declared that nuclear weapons could be used for retaliatory purposes and that there were no religious restrictions on such use. Gharavian said that "based on religious law, everything depends on our purpose".[20] Moreover, Gharavian declared that the decision to "report" rather than "refer" the Iranian nuclear case to the UN Security Council was merely "rhetoric" aimed at intimidating Iran. This was the first time that an Iranian cleric had raised the issue of using nuclear weapons. More importantly, Gharavian's statement called into question Ayatollah Khamene'i's "ruling" regarding nuclear weapons. Gharavian's statement suggested that either a powerful group associated with Mesbah-Yazdi was calling into question Khamene'i's ruling or that Khamene'i had changed his position.

The evidence suggests that Khamene'i had indeed changed his position. The change was enunciated by the supreme jurisconsult's representative on the nuclear issue, Hojjat ol-Eslam Zolnur. Addressing families of martyrs in Karaj and Eshtehard on 18 February 2006, Zolnur said that the world must take Iranian threats seriously, declaring: "In the event of the imposition of economic sanctions, Iran will withdraw from the Non Proliferation Treaty" (NPT).[21] It is unlikely that Khamene'i's representative on nuclear affairs would call for NPT withdrawal without his prior approval.

During this period, there was also speculation that Larijani's position in the leadership had deteriorated.[22] However, the government continued to negotiate with Russia, under Larijani's influence and with Khamene'i's approval. Khamene'i probably sought to prolong the negotiations while increasing Iran's nuclear potential, a policy also known as "talk and build". The point at issue was persuading Iran's interlocutors to agree to uranium enrichment on Iranian territory, and to use their consent as a means of exerting diplomatic leverage on the US.

One of the leaders of the pro-reform Islamic Revolution Mojahedin Organization, Mohsen Armin, lambasted the government for its failure to co-opt the EU-3, arguing that: "The Europeans did not want Iran to be reported to the Security Council. They did not want this case to end like this. In fact, they wanted the problem to be solved through holding talks and negotiations."[23] Armin criticized the Ahmadinezhad government for its threats to pursue non-peaceful nuclear options: "The fact that we announced in an official speech that until today our activities have been peaceful, but don't do anything that will lead us to change our ways, will escalate the crisis."[24] Armin also sharply criticized Ahmadinezhad for his denial of the Holocaust.

Although the reformists and the Rafsanjani camp did not directly criticize Khamene'i, the thrust of their policies left no doubt that they held the supreme leader responsible for Ahmadinezhad's actions. They took two inter-related measures to compel Khamene'i to change his strategy or face removal. The first step was to create a grand coalition consisting of all the political groups in the country that opposed Ahmadinezhad, but did not believe in the violent overthrow of the regime. The second step was to increase the level of support for Rafsanjani in the Assembly of Experts by calling for major changes in the rules governing the Assembly of Experts elections. The first step was a failure in terms of its overall impact on Iranian strategy. The issue of forming "a democratic front" or grand coalition to oppose Ahmadinezhad led to endless debate about the merits of the case. The second step which was far more effective, if only because it immediately led to a backlash, was aimed at discrediting Mesbah-Yazdi and preventing him from mobilizing theological seminaries and the clerical establishment in support of Khamene'i.

Given their fear of revolution or chronic unrest, it is not surprising that Iranian reformists should have concentrated their efforts on weaning key institutions from the supreme leader one by one. This strategy was primarily formulated by Sa'id Hajjarian, who called for moving from "fortress to fortress". The assassination attempt against Hajjarian, which was probably sanctioned by his former colleagues in the Intelligence Ministry led to his temporary removal from the scene. However, since the summer of 2005 he has re-emerged as a key strategist in the reformist camp and he has sought to form a broad coalition against President Ahmadinezhad. Hajjarian has argued that the referral of Iran's nuclear case to the UN Security Council would lead the Ahmadinezhad government to order a crackdown and stifle dissent in the country. Hajjarian went so far as to try to form a grand coalition among the pro-Khatami Islamic Iran Participation Front, the dissident Iran Freedom Movement, the pro-Rafsanjani Executives of Construction Party and the strongly conservative Islamic Coalition Party, which is part of the Ahmadinezhad government.[25] Although such a coalition has not been officially formed, the de facto collaboration among a diverse array of groups opposing Khamenei and Ahmadinezhad's policies has led Khamenei to seek to limit the political influence of Ahmadinezhad and his allies.

Opposition to Mesbah-Yazdi

It has been alleged that Mesbah-Yazdi is a member of Hojjatieh, an allegation that he has rejected.[26] Opposition to Hojjatieh was expressed in Iran's Supreme Court, which has been a bastion of conservatism. A Supreme Court judge Hojjat ol-Eslam Mohammad Sadeq Al-e Eshaq claimed that Hojjatieh still existed and warned of the threat posed by "reactionaries". He accused Hojjatieh of disguising its ulterior motives so that it could enter government.[27]

Others have subjected Mesbah-Yazdi's declarations to close scrutiny in an attempt to demonstrate that he is a mendacious political opportunist. Abdolkarim Sorush's critique of Mesbah-Yazdi's pronouncements is particularly important in view of the fact that he was a member of Hojjatieh. Sorush has contended that some of Ahmadinezhad's key supporters have been influenced by the ideas of Iranian philosopher Ahmad Fardid, who was a prominent interpreter of the works of German philosopher Martin Heidegger. Fardid invented the concept of "Westoxication" which was popularized by another Iranian philosopher, Jalal Al-Ahmad. According to Sorush, Fardid was also responsible for popularizing anti-Semitism. Moreover, he has contended that despite Fardid's lack of religious or revolutionary credentials, he sided with the regime's hard-liners after the revolution. Sorush has declared that Mesbah-Yazdi is far worse than the Taleban because at least the Taleban were sincere in their beliefs. He has said that Mesbah-Yazdi and his supporters will leave the country and the regime to fend for themselves in the event of a confrontation with the West.[28]

Mesbah-Yazdi and his allies, however, continued their efforts to support Khamene'i. What they feared most was that Rafsanjani, who was the deputy Speaker of the Assembly of Experts, would increase his number of supporters in the assembly, which is responsible for selecting Iran's supreme leader, and pose a leadership challenge to Khamene'i, reduce the supreme leader to a figurehead and compel him to change Iran's strategy. Rafsanjani had travelled to Qom and warned senior clerics of "the danger of Ayatollah Mesbah and his pupils becoming powerful".[29]

A source close to Ayatollah Mesbah-Yazdi said that his criteria for supporting Assembly of Experts candidates were as follows: "Belief in a religious government and the presence of religion in various social arenas", "belief in the principle of the guardianship of the supreme jurisconsult", "belief in the exalted Ayatollah Khamene'i as the most honest individual who is a symbol of the guardianship of the supreme jurisconsult", "being in harmony with the exalted Ayatollah Khamene'i's ideas", "belief in social justice" and "lacking the inclination to support Hashemi-Rafsanjani".[30] Indeed, a source close to Mesbah-Yazdi said: "If the nominees have all the required qualifications but they also support Mr Hashemi-Rafsanjani they will not be supported by us."[31]

By summer 2006 it was clear to Iranian officials that it was only a matter of time before the US would move to impose sanctions on their country.[32] It was during this period that Khamene'i made a speech declaring that Iran would be willing to share its nuclear technology with other nations.[33] Khamenei also moved to consolidate his own domestic position while threatening to play the energy card internationally. At the time, Japan, which was considering the possibility of curtailing the remittances of Iranian workers in Japan, as well as other sanctions against Iran[34], seems to have been the main target of Iranian threats. While North Korea was threatening to conduct missile tests, Khamene'i warned that any US threats against Iran would endanger world energy supplies. Khamene'i declared that Iran did not pose a threat to anyone, adding that Iran had good relations with European countries, which needed Iran's gas, as well as with Russia, Asian and Arab countries. He also made it clear that, from his point of view, Iran and Russia a had "common interests" in Central Asia and the Middle East. He then declared that US could not secure world energy supplies: "In order to threaten Iran, you (America) say that you can secure the energy flow in the region. You are wrong." Khamenei said that Iran would "never start a war" and that its only intention was to "build an Iran which provides this nation with moral and material prosperity". "We want an Iran that can be a role-model for all other nations."[35]

By now Khamenei knew that Ahmadinezhad's policies were endangering his own domestic position. The dispute over the choice of strategy was so closely intertwined with the issue of Khamene'i's leadership that it was difficult to resolve one issue without the other. Khamene'i tried to de-link the two issues in July when he formed a foreign policy co-ordination council. Almost immediately, there were contradictory statements by senior Iranian officials on the functions and responsibilities of the council. One group of officials argued that the council would only define the parameters of policy and refrain from interfering in the implementation of policy and strategy. Others, most notably those who had just been asked to serve on the council, argued that the council would in effect formulate Iranian strategy.[36]

The evidence suggests that Khamene'i was involved in a complex manoeuvre to consolidate his own domestic power base which was being increasingly threatened by the Rafsanjani-Khatami-Rowhani triumvirate. The most significant move during this period was the crackdown on Hojjatieh.[37] Another significant policy decision by Khamenei during this period was a directive to ensure that the government would implement privatization programmes and integrate the country into the world economy. Khamenei's directive would necessitate a "change in the role of government from one of ownership and direct management to an agency for supervision and policymaking."[38] This was undoubtedly a major setback for Ahmadinezhad who had been the most prominent advocate of wealth redistribution and helping "the dispossessed" in the country. It was also a major concession to the right-of-centre Rafsanjani-Rowhani group, as well as to the Islamic Coalition Party.

It seems that Khamenei's main objective was to limit Ahmadinezhad's powers in the domestic policy arena, while harnessing his radicalism to increase the geopolitical pressure on Israel and the US. Thus, on the Middle Eastern front, the Iranian government stepped up its propaganda campaign aimed at provoking Israel to react viscerally, which the president seemed to believe would lead to such regional instability that it would inevitably limit the scope of an Israeli or US attack on Iran's nuclear installations.

However, the main difference of opinion among Iranian leaders was over how far Iran could escalate without endangering the existence of the Iranian regime itself. President Ahmadinezhad probably sought to prolong the Lebanese crisis to maximize regional instability and to provoke a premature Israeli reaction in the hopes of gaining leverage in the nuclear negotiations or to gain a casus belli to prepare the ground for Iran's withdrawal from the NPT. The head of the Expediency Council Akbar Hashemi-Rafsanjani sought to broker a cease-fire only a few days after the outbreak of the conflict probably in the hopes of preparing the ground for talks with the US, which he had long favoured, as well as of undermining Ahmadinezhad whose political fortune by now was closely tied to the pursuit of radical policies. The secretary of the Supreme National Security Council Ali Larijani was undoubtedly closer to the Rafsanjani line as far as foreign policy was concerned, but he would find it difficult to challenge the president head-on without precipitating a major domestic political crisis.[39] Given the complexity of the leadership and foreign policy issues, it is not surprising that Khamenei should have sought to protect himself by creating a foreign policy council to shield him from criticism.[40]

However, different threat perceptions also led to different levels of support for escalation. That was probably the main reason why when President Ahmadinezhad inaugurated the heavy water project at Arak he declared that the Iranian nuclear programme did not pose a threat to anyone, including Israel.[41] It soon became clear that the statement did not reflect Ahmadinezhad's own thinking. During his visit to the US, Ahmadinezhad continued to try to provoke Israel.[42] Significantly, during the same period, the deputy Speaker of Majlis, Mohammad Reza Bahonar, declared that if the pressure on Iran increased, then "the Iranian people" would ask the government to withdraw from the NPT and produce nuclear weapons "for the sake of deterrence".[43]

Moreover, after the Lebanese conflict it became increasingly clear that Hezbollah would not be prepared to confront the US. Thus Iran increasingly relied upon Venezuela and North Korea as potential allies that could challenge the US in asymmetric political warfare in their own neighbourhoods.[44]

However, Ahmadinezhad's opponents sought to revive the strategy of selective cooperation with the US on Iraq and Afghanistan. The assumption on which this strategy was based was that the deteriorating political situation in Iraq and Afghanistan would lead the US to tacitly agree to the continuation of uranium enrichment and plutonium separation on Iranian territory as part of a regional solution which would also entail the recognition of Iran as a regional power. The Iranian leadership undoubtedly attempted to convey this message to the West during Mohammad Khatami's visits to the US and the UK. During those visits Khatami sharply criticized US policy, arguing that it had actually increased terrorism around the world. During his visit to the UK, Khatami declared that the US had been defeated in Iraq and Afghanistan and characterized US policy as "a joke".[45] However, there were hints that Khatami represented that cross-section of the Iranian state which was willing to negotiate with the US on Iraq and Afghanistan.

In October 2006, however, the Iranian policy of constructing a second tier of hostile states opposed to US policy suffered serious set-backs. First Iran cancelled the contract with the Japanese company INPEX to develop its Azadegan oilfield. Negotiations had been prolonged and the Iranians believed that the Japanese were stalling because of their close alliance with the US.[46] This indicated that Japan did not give priority to its energy supplies over its alliance with the US on non-proliferation issues. Secondly, Iran's North Korea option backfired. Instead of driving a wedge between the US and Japan, the North Korean missile and nuclear tests brought the two countries closer. They discussed the deployment of ballistic missile defence systems to counter the North Korean threat.[47]

The regional military exercises under the aegis of the Proliferation Security Initiative led to contradictory reactions in Iran, if only because of the persisting disagreements over the choice of strategy. The participation of Gulf Cooperation Council states as well as South Korea, albeit as an observer, indicated that the Bush administration was capable of forming a regional coalition to challenge Iranian regional strategy. The participation of South Korea also suggested that there would be an effort to halt the shipment of WMD-related material to Iran via North Korea.[48] However, the deteriorating political situation in Iraq seems to have convinced Khamenei that a total change of regional strategy was not needed despite the set-backs Iran encountered.

Rafsanjani challenges Khamenei's leadership

Rafsanjani moved against Ahmadinezhad's main protector, Ayatollah Khamene'i, raising the issue of Khamene'i's leadership and indeed of Iran's system of government, arguing that there had been a debate about forming a council of jurisconsults. Moreover, Rafsanjani argued that one of the most important responsibilities of the Assembly of Experts was to supervise the activities of the supreme leader and "some work is being carried out on this issue".[49] Although Rafsanjani said that he disagreed with direct elections for the supreme leader[50], his comments on the importance of supervising the activities of the supreme leader were fully consistent with the views of those pro-reform politicians who favoured the curtailment of Khamenei's powers. Rafsanjani was immediately attacked by Ahmadinezhad's supporters among the Islamic Revolutionary Guards Corps, who accused him of betraying the revolution and corruption. They also accused his sons of corruption, arguing that Rafsanjani had been lying about his sons' economic activities.[51] Moreover, the newspaper Partowe Sokhan, which reflects the views of Ayatollah Mesbah-Yazdi, published a letter from Iranian seminarians who sharply criticized Rafsanjani for weakening the theocratic system.[52]

Clearly, the debate was not just about methods of electing the supreme jurisconsult. The crux of the matter was the dispute over nuclear policy and regional strategy and Rafsanjani was signalling that, as far as he was concerned, the issue of Khamenei's leadership was closely intertwined with the dispute. Rafsanjani responded to his critics by revealing a letter written to Khomeyni in the latter stages of the Iran-Iraq war, by the then commander-in chief of the Islamic Revolutionary Guards Corps, Mohsen Reza'i, arguing that Iran had to acquire nuclear weapons in order to defeat Iraq.[53] Clearly, Rafsanjani's objective was to argue that the Guards were guilty of opposing the supreme leader, since the supreme leader had said that the pursuit of nuclear weapons was un-Islamic.[54] The ensuing controversy led Reza'i to hint that he had written the letter on Rafsanjani's behalf.[55] Rafsanjani's action brought opprobrium upon him. President Ahmadinezhad criticized him for "undermining confidence in the country's abilities" during the war.[56] Moreover, a number of commentators who were supporters of Ahmadinezhad, such as Hoseyn Shari'atmadari, the managing-editor of the radical daily Kayhan, sharply criticized both Rafsanjani and Reza'i.[57]

Rafsanjani's supporters, however, described the letter as a warning to those whose extremist policies were likely to endanger the country.[58] Rafsanjani's challenge to Ahmadinezhad's foreign policy occurred at a bad time for Khamenei, because by early October he was also facing a serious domestic challenge to his authority.

Clerical opposition to the rule of the supreme jurisconsult had been an undercurrent of Iranian politics since the inception of the Islamic Republic. In the 1980s Grand Ayatollah Seyyed Kazem Shari'atmadari had been defrocked because of his opposition to Ayatollah Khomeyni's doctrine of the guardianship of the supreme jurisconsult. In the 1990s and the first decade of the 21st century, a number of prominent reformist clerics such as Yusefi-Eshkevari and Mohsen Kadivar had raised serious questions about the rule of the supreme jurisconsult. Eshkevari was also defrocked because of his opposition to Ayatollah Ali Khamenei.[59] The most prominent clerical opponent of Khamenei has been Grand Ayatollah Hoseyn Ali Montazeri, who was Khomeyni's official deputy before being ostracized and put under house arrest. Montazeri has sharply criticized despotic rule and violation of human rights in Iran.

By October 2006, Ayatollah Hoseyn Kazemeyni-Borujerdi had emerged as one of the fiercest critics of Iran's theocracy, raising profound questions about the theological foundations of the regime, thereby calling into question the authority of Iran's supreme leader. According to one report, Kazemeyni-Borujerdi's supporters claimed that their leader had received instructions from the Hidden Imam to call for the separation of religion and politics.[60]

Above all, Kazemeyni-Borujerdi challenged those who claimed that the Iranian regime had received its authority from God. This position was expressed explicitly by the secretary of the Assembly of Experts, Ayatollah Ali Meshkini, who declared: "The Islamic Republic is the continuation of God on earth... Thus any disobedience of its rules amounts to a revolt against God."[61] Kazemeyni-Borujerdi accused the regime of turning people "away from God" because of repression, discrimination and pressure.[62] He said that in the last 14 years he has been summoned on "numerous occasions" to the Special Clerical Court, that he was jailed in 1995 and arrested several times in 2001. (Since taking over as supreme leader in 1989, Khamenei has used the Special Clerical Court to punish his clerical opponents.) He blamed the regime for the death of his father under "suspicious circumstances" in 2002, and said that two of his mosques had been "confiscated" and that dozens of his supporters had been arrested and imprisoned in Evin Prison. Borujerdi has called for assistance from prominent figures such as the Pope and EU foreign policy chief Javier Solana.[63]

According to Borujerdi, the pressure on him and his followers increased after "thousands of people" attended a meeting he had organized on 30 June 2006. He claimed that the regime had staged "a coup d'état" against him because it feared that otherwise "millions of people" would rally around him.[64] Borujerdi was strongly supported by the son of Grand Ayatollah Kazem Shari'atmadari, Hasan Shari'atmadari, who lives in exile in Germany. According to Hasan Shari'atmadari many Iranian clerics are potential supporters of Borujerdi, but they do not dare to express their views openly for fear of being persecuted by the regime. According to Shari'atmadari the regime had decided to crackdown on Borujerdi's activities because it feared that other clerics might follow in his footsteps.[65]

Borujerdi said that "in recent weeks" more than 100 people had been arrested, jailed and tortured, that others had lost their jobs and others had been pressured to campaign against him. According to Amnesty International, at least 41 of Borujerdi's supporters had been arrested in his courtyard.[66] Reportedly, Borujerdi was taken into custody in October 2006.[67]

The Elections

The decision to hold Assembly of Experts and council elections simultaneously had been extremely controversial in Iran. Deputy interior minister for political affairs Ali Jannati changed the vetting rules for the assembly significantly when he declared that henceforward the Basij Resistance Force would informally vet candidates. Jannati's argument was that the Interior Ministry and the legislature lacked the necessary means to supervise the elections and that, therefore, the Basij was the only trustworthy organ of state which could do so.

Jannati's policy caused a firestorm of protest in the ranks of reformists who contended that the decision to hold the elections simultaneously was aimed at ensuring the reformists' defeat. It also demonstrated that Ahmadinezhad's supporters were determined to tighten their hold on power. Jannati's father, Ahmad

Jannati, the speaker of the Guardian Council, which is responsible for vetting candidates and ensuring that legislation is consistent with Islamic law, had been a bête noire of reformists throughout Khatami's presidency. He was among a handful of senior clerics who ardently supported Ahmadinezhad. Jannati claimed that his candidacy for the Assembly of Experts and his responsibility for vetting the candidates did not mean that he had a conflict of interest.[68] Nevertheless, Jannati's son, Ali, was replaced as deputy interior minister for political affairs and appointed as Iranian ambassador to Kuwait. His successor, Mojtaba Samareh-Hashemi (sometimes mistakenly called Hashemi-Samareh), had served as the head of Ahmadinezhad's office and was very close to Ayatollah Mesbah-Yazdi.[69] His appointment meant that a strong supporter of Mesbah-Yazdi would be in charge of supervising the elections, thereby denying Rafsanjani the opportunity to gain control of the Assembly of Experts. These moves indicated that Ahmadinezhad was working closely with Mesbah-Yazdi to prevent Rafsanjani from establishing himself as co-jurisconsult.

However, Ahmadinezhad's political alliances and the failure of his economic policies led critics to accuse him of cronyism and incompetence. Particularly significant was the government's failure to deliver on economic promises to help "the dispossessed".[70] By now dissidents and reformists were referring to Ahmadinezhad and his radical allies as "the hidden garrison party". They were also concerned that once they had finished with Rafsanjani, Ahmadinezhad and his allies in the Guards and the clerical establishment would target other prominent "revolutionary clerics".[71] They also held the Ahmadinezhad government responsible for the escalation of tensions with the US. Indeed the web site Baztab, which is close to the secretary of the Expediency Council, Mohsen Reza'i, published a report saying that in addition to attacking Iran's nuclear installations, the naval forces deployed near Iran would also attack Iran's military installations, "terrorist-training camps", air defence systems, medium-range ballistic missiles, submarines and warships. In this scenario, war would be over after five days.[72]

The Assembly of Experts elections were the acid test of the Khatami-Rafsanjani-Rowhani triumvirate's ability to undermine Khamene'i's leadership. Dissatisfaction with Ahmadinezhad's economic policies seems to have led Khamenei to try to manoeuvre himself into a position between Ahmadinezhad and his opponents. Significantly, at a meeting with Ahmadinezhad and his cabinet, Khamenei called on the government to "eliminate inflation" and to understand that "serving the people necessitates refraining from getting involved in peripheral matters and political factionalism".[73] However, in public Khamenei strongly defended Ahmadinezhad, in November 2006 describing the opponents of the government as foreign agents.[74]

The fact that Ahmadinezhad had to appoint the hardest of hard-liners to gain control of the Interior Ministry spoke volumes about his narrow power base in the Iranian establishment. Ahmadinezhad had set up an election committee headed by Sadeq Mahsuli. Moreover, he named Mahsuli as his representative to the committee to coordinate the activities of "the fundamentalists".[75] However, apparently Ahmadinezhad made exorbitant demands which would have led to the elimination of the co-ordination council and would have enabled him and his close advisers to supervise the election campaign. Reportedly, the president's representative had also threatened the fundamentalists that if they resisted the president's demands, they would be de-selected.[76] However, reportedly, "senior officials" intervened and "banned the president, ministers and vice-presidents from interfering in the elections".[77]

Only Ayatollah Khamenei was powerful enough to prevent the president and the cabinet from interfering in the elections. Reportedly, "the president's entourage had tried to deny that such a ban existed and sought to pursue their electoral activities through other channels".[78] However, Khamenei probably persuaded the Guardian Council, which is responsible for vetting candidates, to disqualify a large number of radicals in the elections, thereby ensuring the defeat of many pro-Ahmadinezhad radicals.[79] What prevented Khamenei from siding with Ahmadinezhad in the elections was apparently his assessment of the likely risks associated with fully embracing the Ahmadinezhad programme.

In fact, by now, Ahmadinezhad was so unpopular that when he visited Amir Kabir University a group of students chanted slogans against him and set fire to his posters.[80] Ahmadinezhad later wrote about his experience in his weblog. He claimed that as a "university student" he had "repeatedly fought and escaped from the Shah's violent police".

"I remembered what a heavy price one had to pay for even mildly criticizing the state. Yesterday, when I saw this example of freedom in action, I, Mahmud Ahmadinezhad, did not feel the least bit hurt by anyone. In fact, as the servant of this nation and the president and official responsible for managing the political affairs of this country, I was truly proud of this great revolution which gave us freedom and I thanked God."[81]

However, Ali Azizi, the deputy secretary of the Islamic Association of the Students of Amir Kabir University said that the students previously had been attacked by the Basij Resistance Force and that the building housing the Islamic association of students had been bulldozed at night. He said that it was inconceivable that members of the Force would attack students without Ahmadinezhad's permission, adding that the students had the "right to retaliate", but "because we do not support violence, the students only set fire to his posters".[82] Subsequently, a group of students calling themselves "the real polytechnic students" wrote an open later to Ahmadinezhad sharply criticizing him for the brutal treatment and suspension of students during his presidency.[83]

Moreover, the demonstrations also exposed the divisions in the ranks of pro-Khatami reformists. The general-secretary of the Islamic Iran Participation Front, Mohsen Mirdamadi, who had sharply criticized Ahmadinezhad's foreign policy, criticized the students, arguing that "the people had elected Ahmadinezhad".[84] Mirdamadi's remarks came as a shock because until then the Party's official position was that Ahmadinezhad's government was "a garrison government" created as a result of the activities of "the hidden government and vote-rigging".[85] Subsequently, the deputy general-secretary of the party, Abdollah Ramezanzadeh, apologized to the students for Mirdamadi's remarks. Ramezanzadeh also contended that Ahmadinezhad had gone to Amir Kabir University to campaign for his allies in the elections.[86] The demonstrations occurred at a particularly bad time for Ahmadinezhad. The fact that Iran's state-run media showed students setting fire to his posters demonstrated that his political influence was rapidly declining in the eyes of Iran's supreme leader.

Faced with the prospect of a narrower power base as a result of the increasing opposition to Ahmadinezhad, Khamenei began to prepare the ground for curtailing Ahmadinezhad's powers and broadening his own power base. In the run-up to the elections, the president was challenged by a coalition of conservatives in the Majlis, who sought to shorten his term of office. The main challenge came from a conservative coalition led by Ahmad Tavakkoli and Elias Naderan, both at the radical end of the conservative spectrum in Iranian politics. Naderan's involvement was particularly significant given his close ties to the Islamic Revolutionary Guards Corps.[87]

The debate over the nature of Iran's leadership came to a head shortly before the elections. Not surprisingly, the protagonists in the debate were Sa'id Hajjarian and Ayatollah Mesbah-Yazdi. Hajjarian asked what the Assembly of Experts would do if the leader and the assembly were in disagreement. Would the leader dissolve the assembly or would the assembly remove the leader? Ayatollah Mesbah-Yazdi argued that one had to consider the context. He argued that if the leader chose to dissolve the assembly he could do so provided that his decision preceded that of the assembly. Hajjarian, however, disagreed sharply, arguing that since the ayatollah believed that the supreme leader had received his powers from God, the Assembly of Experts was in no position to challenge the supreme jurisconsult because it was a mere earthling.[88]

The debate brought the issue of republicanism versus theocracy to a head just prior to the elections. Rafsanjani represented those who were trying to reduce the supreme jurisconsult to a mere earthling, whereas Ahmadinezhad and his supporters had already made a bargain with Khamene'i, total political support in return for a break with the traditional conservatives and reformists on nuclear policy and regional strategy. The radicals were to be disappointed. The results of the elections indicated that their power base was too narrow.

The radicals' defeat in the elections in December 2006 was a major set-back for Khamene'i and Ahmadinezhad. All of the key positions in the Interior Ministry, which is responsible for supervising the holding of the elections, were held by Ahmadinezhad's supporters. Yet they failed to prevent their candidates from being defeated, largely because they had failed to deliver on their promises and had alienated much of the clerical establishment. The results also demonstrated that Ayatollah Khamene'i had failed to exploit Ahmadinezhad's radicalism to broaden his own power base on the basis of a new pact between himself and young radicals – sometimes described as Iranian neo-conservatives. That was why Khamenei changed his domestic political strategy and sought to consolidate his domestic power base by curtailing Ahmadinezhad's powers.

Nevertheless, Ahmadinezhad behaved as though his coalition had not been defeated. His supporters sought to portray the elections as a victory for the Iranian people by drawing attention to the high turn-out. They blamed the reformists for alienating the people while arguing that turn-out had increased as a result of the president's policies. Pro-Ahmadinezhad media outlets had very little to say about the political affiliations of those who won the elections.

Foreign policy and the disarray in Iran's leadership

As the results of the elections were being announced, the Iranian government began to take measures in anticipation of US moves against Iran. The failure of its economic policies had caused a lack of confidence in Iran's stock exchange. Nine months into Ahmadinezhad's presidency Tehran Stock Exchange reached its lowest point.[89] However, this did not stop the regime from trying to challenge the dollar. The announcement of the shift from the dollar to the euro in oil transactions in December 2006 was undoubtedly aimed at undermining the dollar at a time when the US was negotiating with China on currency and trade issues.[90] The move was also combined with efforts to negotiate energy agreements with China, India and Pakistan in an effort to pressure the US into changing its regional strategy. Despite the growing concern about Iran's possible use of the oil weapon to retaliate against Western sanctions, sceptics argued that this would hurt Iran far more than the US or the West because oil was the mainstay of the country's economy.[91]

The Iranian government had also begun to prepare itself for the imposition of sanctions on Iran. As early as November 2005, Iranian Oil Minister Vaziri-Hamaneh called for OPEC production cuts. One factor which undoubtedly influenced the thinking of Iranian officials was the declining fortunes of the Iraqi oil industry.[92] The energy situation was further complicated in January 2006 due to unrest in Nigeria and the Russo-Ukrainian gas dispute.[93] There were fears that Iran could respond to Western pressure on its nuclear programme by cutting back its daily sale of 2.4 million barrels of oil.[94] Saudi Arabia, which was undoubtedly deeply concerned about the Iranian nuclear programme, promised to produce more oil if needed, adding that OPEC was likely to keep its output steady.[95]

Former deputy Minister of Economy and Finance Mohsen Safa'i-Farahani made it clear that the country could end up bankrupting itself in the process. A Johns Hopkins University report released in late December 2006 indicated that Iran's energy position was worse than even the worst-case scenario envisaged by most sceptics. According to the study, given Iran's increasing domestic consumption, the country would probably cease to export oil by 2015.[96] While not ruling out the possibility that Iran was pursuing a nuclear weapons programme, the study contended that there were sound economic reasons for the country's pursuit of a nuclear programme to generate energy.[97]

Ahmadinezhad suffered a defeat when the anti-Holocaust conference did not engender sufficient support for the Iranian regime to prevent a de facto accommodation between Israel and conservative Arab states on the issue of the Iranian nuclear programme. Indeed conservative Arab states were increasingly formulating their foreign policies on the assumption that Israel was part of the Middle Eastern state system, whereas the Iranian regime was trying to overturn that system to impose its hegemony on the region. Saudi Arabia in particular seemed to be increasingly convinced that Iran was positioning itself as the only alternative to the US in the region.[98] Speaking in an interview with a Kuwaiti newspaper, King Abdullah of Saudi Arabia declared that Iranian policies posed a threat to the region. He also expressed concern about Shi'i proselytising.[99] The Saudis also responded by encouraging Iraqi Sunni guerrillas who were fighting Iranian-backed Iraqi Shi'i groups, such as the Supreme Council for Islamic Revolution in Iraq.[100]

This might have offered the Iranian regime an opportunity to explore the possibility of reaching an accommodation with the US, given the concerns in Washington about the Saudi policy. Instead Ahmadinezhad's Holocaust denial policy dealt a severe blow to Iran's efforts to cultivate Western think tanks and academic institutions, a policy which pre-dated even the Khatami government. The Iranian Foreign Ministry think tank which organized the Holocaust denial conference was boycotted by 40 prominent Western think tanks and academic institutions.[101]

The Iranian president was increasingly viewed as a radical who was determined to destroy Israel and spread radicalism throughout the Middle East and the Islamic world. Even some Iranian conservatives who were rather hawkish on the nuclear issue seem to have been alarmed at the prospect of the regime's international isolation as a result of its pursuit of such extremist policies.[102] The fact that some reformist commentators were allowed to appear on the country's state-run media[103] to argue their case suggested that Ayatollah Khamenei, who appoints the head of the state-run media, was hedging his bets.

Former nuclear negotiator Hoseyn Musavian predicted the imposition of economic sanctions on Iran and called for "flexibility, caution and patience", as well as negotiations.[104] Perhaps the most serious criticism of Ahmadinezhad's policies was voiced by former Iranian senior diplomat Ali Khorram who argued that the UN Security Council resolution meant that Iran was now "on the same level as North Korea, which possesses nuclear weapons".[105]

However, Ahmadinezhad refused to retreat. Appearing before the Majlis to present his budget bill, the Iranian president declared that the UN Security Council resolution against Iran was "still born" and that more resolutions would not work.[106] Ahmadinezhad declared that military threats would prove ineffective, as they had been before, for example when Iran opened its nuclear installations in Esfahan.[107]

However, the threat of US military action was taken very seriously in Iran. For example, Mohsen Reza'i, former commander-in-chief of the Islamic Revolutionary Guards Corps and the current secretary of the Expediency Council, declared that the US reason for arresting Iranians in Iraq was to "provide a documentary pretext and find a reason for attacking Iran". Reza'i said that President Bush "had taken the possibility of defeat very seriously". "We must not resort to adventurism and irrational acts."[108]

On the whole, there seemed to be a difference of opinion between Iranian conservative and radical commentators over the best form of deterrence against the US. Conservatives primarily raised the issue of the threat to oil supplies. A number of conservative Iranian MPs, most notably the chairman of the Majlis National Security and Foreign Policy Committee, Ala'eddin Borujerdi, and chairman of the Majlis Energy Committee Kamal Daneshyar, warned that in the event of a confrontation with the US, Iran could endanger the flow of oil through the Persian Gulf.[109] Ahmadinezhad and his allies, however, seemed to favour a confrontation with the US in the belief that Iran had a window of opportunity to exploit what they considered to be Iranian escalation dominance in Iraq, Afghanistan and the region. They assumed that a confrontation with Israel would make it difficult for Sunni-majority Arab states, whose regimes they believed had been delegitimated as the result of the Iraq war, to join US and Israel in a war with Iran. Their strategic thinking assumed that military action against Iran would be politically costly for the US because it would bring down the US' Arab allies.

The managing-editor of Kayhan, Hoseyn Shari'atmadari, who had continued to call for Iran's withdrawal from the NPT, provided the most detailed account of such thinking in radical circles. In a 22 January editorial titled, "Is there going to be a war?", Shari'atmadari declared that the threat of US military action was part of a "psychological warfare" campaign against Iran. "The Americans must be warned of the terrible consequences that await them and their allies should they act foolishly." US troops stationed to the east and west of Iran's borders "are within range of our fire". When "the powerful missiles are launched from Iran, Israel will become a scorching hell for the Zionists before they reach actual hell".[110] He listed a number of measures that the Iranian regime might take in response to US action, such as disrupting the flow of approximately "24 million of the 30 million barrels of oil produced daily by OPEC" through the Strait of Hormuz. He warned: "Some of the Arab states in the region... will not only face a large economic and social crisis – their very existence will be seriously endangered."[111]

On 28 January, Shari'atmadari sharply criticized the UN's adoption of a resolution condemning any denial of the Holocaust.[112] Shari'atmadari wrote that the Holocaust was "a myth" and "an excuse" used by the West "to establish the illegal Zionist regime". "The resolution prepares the UN's corpse for burial in the graveyard of history".[113] In another editorial published on 5 February, Kayhan raised the spectre of a regional conflagration in the event of an attack on Iran, warning: "NATO forces in Afghanistan, the US Fifth Fleet in Bahrain, the British troops in southern Iraq, and every element identified with the American camp will clearly see his death before his eyes."[114]

However, the Iranian Defence Ministry and the Guards primarily issued threats that left something to chance. Speaking in an interview with Al-Wefaq newspaper (published by Iran's Cultural Press Institution), Najjar declared: "Military action against Iran is tantamount to suicide." While ruling out "any sort of military confrontation", Najjar warned: "If our nuclear facilities come under attack we will react seriously and resolutely and respond to any aggression against Iran's territory in such a way as to make them regret."[115] Similar statements were made by the Commander-in-Chief of the Revolutionary Guards Corps, Major-General Yahya Rahim-Safavi.[116]

Throughout January and the first half of February, the Iranian president dismissed talk of military action against Iran, while claiming that the US lacked the necessary capability. At the same time, some of Ahmadinezhad's closest political allies stepped up their anti-Israel campaign.[117] The linkage between the anti-NPT and Holocaust denial policy was most explicit in the comments of Hoseyn Shari'atmadari and Mohammad Ali Ramin. Ramin, who was also the head of the political bureau of the pro-Ahmadinezhad faction, The Sweet Scent of Service, admitted that he had been raising the issue of the Holocaust in the last 10 years via various media outlets. However, he denied that he was an adviser to Ahmadinezhad. Ramin sharply escalated the political war with Israel by describing Adolf Hitler as a Jew. He said that the reason for Hitler's anti-Semitism was that Hitler's mother was "a Jewish prostitute".[118] Moreover, Ramin explicitly stated that there was a link between the Holocaust denial policy and Iran's tactics in the nuclear negotiations. Ramin contended that since the revolution the West had been criticizing Iran for lack of democracy and human rights violations, including the violation of the rights of women. According to Ramin, holding the conference on the Holocaust had enabled Iran to reverse the trend. Moreover, Ramin linked the Holocaust denial policy to the issue of extending Iran's security perimeter to Lebanon and Palestinian areas, contending:

> "By raising such issues we should try to define our national interests by looking beyond our geographical borders. Today, no country can define its security within its own borders. So, for example, if we define our security perimeter within the boundaries of Lebanon and Palestine, then, naturally, we will be able to provide ourselves with an additional internal security guarantee."[119]

One of the main architects of this concept of security without frontiers was Hasan Abbasi, a former Revolutionary Guards commander and staunch supporter of President Ahmadinezhad.

The fact that Ahmadinezhad and his allies continued to pursue the Holocaust denial policy even in the face of opposition by prominent Iranian conservatives who were hawkish on the nuclear issue suggests that they were trying to provoke an Israeli attack on Iran to settle the debate over the choice of strategy. Press reports indeed said that Israel was preparing for attacking Iranian nuclear installations and that, if necessary, Israel would use nuclear weapons to destroy those installations.[120] Israel denied that it was preparing for such an attack.[121] The Iranian Foreign Ministry issued a statement saying that Iran would retaliate immediately in the event of such an attack.[122] However, the Foreign Ministry issued another statement, saying that Iran would continue to cooperate with the IAEA. Significantly, even the Majlis committee set up to review Iran's cooperation with the IAEA declared that it would do so within the framework of the NPT. Iran's chief nuclear negotiator Ali Larijani declared that Iran would "continue" its "cooperation with the IAEA" on the basis of the NPT.[123]

Thus despite the UN resolution against Iran and Ahmadinezhad's attempts to cause a major provocation, proponents of the NPT withdrawal option could not carry the day. Iranian Foreign Minister Manuchehr Mottaki was criticized in Iran for describing Iran as "a nuclear country".[124] Larijani's brother, Mohammad Javad Larijani, also argued that "talks on Iran's nuclear issue can continue" only "if Iran is accepted as a nuclear country". Asked whether Russia and China would accept a nuclear Iran, Larijani responded that "the country's foreign policy is not based only on the support of those two states". According to Larijani: "Russia and China do not wish to see Iran possess nuclear weapons, but there is no reason for their opposition to a nuclear Iran." According to Larijani, Russia and China had "declared that they are seeking a nuclear Iran".[125] The Iranian Foreign Ministry had pointed out that Iran was not trying to acquire a nuclear weapons capability. This was also an indirect criticism of President Ahmadinezhad himself since he had earlier declared that the West would not be able to prevent Iran from becoming "a nuclear country". The president's use of the term undoubtedly raised the spectre of changing Iran's declaratory policy and Iran's withdrawal from the NPT, which officials found unacceptable.

Khamenei, however, was the final arbiter. He once again sought to limit Ahmadinezhad's involvement in the nuclear issue. Following a series of foreign reports that he was either dead or dying, Khamenei addressed the people outside his residence in Qom on 8 January 2007. He made it clear that Iran would continue its nuclear programme which he described as "home-grown" and "a source of national pride". He also made it clear that he expected international and domestic pressure to increase.[126]

An editorial in the ultra-conservative daily, Jomhuri-ye Eslami, which usually reflects Khamenei's views, accused Ahmadinezhad of making contradictory and ill-thought-out remarks about the nuclear issue.[127] The editorial blamed Ahmadinezhad for using "aggressive" language and "inappropriate words", suggesting that, as far as the nuclear issue was concerned, he was "obstinate". It also blamed Ahmadinezhad for focusing on the nuclear issue "to cover up" his "government's failures and problems". It strongly advised Ahmadinezhad to follow Khamenei's advice, warning that the nuclear issue transcended political and governmental loyalties: "By referring to the nuclear conflict in your speeches, you have turned it into the symbol and motto of your government. This is not right." It warned Ahmadinezhad that "governments come and go while national issues remain. Just as Iran's territorial integrity, the Persian language, and our Islamic identity are not linked to any particular government, neither is the nuclear issue".[128] The editorial then reminded Ahmadinezhad that the most important aspect of the nuclear programme was "technological progress" and the president had to ensure that he would not "raise the price" that "the nation" had to pay.

"The people need to feel that the president intends to resolve this issue in a sensible manner. The fact that you attach no importance to whether or not the sanctions resolution is passed – that is not the right approach in our opinion. The people are resilient and patient. However, the current sanctions resolution does undoubtedly damage the country."

It blamed Ahmadinezhad for the situation in which Iran found itself, saying that as a result of his attitude the sanctions would be "considerably" expanded.[129] Finally, the editorial urged Ahmadinezhad "to devote time to the nuclear issue only at large national ceremonies. You should not speak too much about this issue in the various districts. Then it made clear that Larijani would be responsible for dealing with the issue, saying that Ahmadinezhad should allow officials in charge of the nuclear "dossier" "to take a stand on "the hooliganism of the Americans and the Westerners".[130]

Jomhuri-ye Eslami also accused him of failing to deliver on his economic promises. However, it also advised the opponents of the government to be "ethical".[131] Criticisms of his policies also surfaced in a letter signed by 150 MPs criticizing him for failing to submit a budget on time and for spending too much time abroad.[132] Moreover, there was a growing rift between Ahmadinezhad and much of the clerical establishment.[133]

By early February Ahmadinezhad was hinting that Khamenei was the final arbiter on the nuclear issue and that he formulated "the general policies" of the state while the government was responsible for implementing them.[134] He also continued to downplay the threat of a US military attack on Iran. It seemed that as far as Khamenei was concerned, Ahmadinezhad's role in nuclear statecraft was to serve as an instrument of fine-tuning Iranian coercive diplomacy in case the Iranian regime had to increase the political and military pressure against the US and its allies. Ahmadinezhad's other role was to co-opt and cultivate the leaders of the so-called "independent states", who were likely to oppose US policy towards Iran. Thus in January 2007 he toured Latin America and his itinerary included meetings with Venezuelan President Hugo Chavez and Nicaraguan President Daniel Ortega. Ahmadinezhad and Chavez pledged to set up a fund worth 2 billion dollars to support countries which opposed US foreign policy.[135]

During this period pressure on Iran increased after the arrest of six Iranians in Arbil, in Iraqi Kurdistan, and with the deployment of a second aircraft carrier strike force and Patriot anti-missile systems in the Persian Gulf.[136] US Defence Secretary Robert Gates said that the Iranians believed that the US was mired down in Iraq and that this meant that "they are in a position to press us in many ways".[137] Gates' statement reflected correctly the perceptions of those who were close to Khamenei. President Ahmadinezhad repeatedly declared that neither Israel nor the US would dare attack Iran. But Khamenei seems to have authorized Larijani to tentatively explore the possibility of a suspension of enrichment in talks with EU foreign policy chief Javier Solana.[138] During Larijani's visit to Saudi Arabia, it was reported that he had asked Saudi Arabia to mediate between the US and Iran, though the Iranians and Saudis denied this.[139]

Khamenei's choice of strategy was becoming increasingly clear by mid February 2007. It was based on the assumption that strategic ties with Russia would enable Iran to maintain a break-out capability. Khamenei increasingly saw Russia as a counterweight to the US on issues of global strategy, as well as to Saudi Arabia in the energy sector. Speculation was rife in the Gulf Cooperation Council states that the US would attack Iran before April because that would enable the US to rely on the support of British Prime Minister Tony Blair.[140]

Iranian Foreign Minister Manuchehr Mottaki accused the UK of encouraging sectarianism, claiming: "London's new strategy now is to foment discord among Shiite and Sunni Muslims in Iraq...other states of the Muslim world."[141] Other Iranian leaders, most notably Khamenei, Rafsanjani and Ahmadinezhad would make similar statements about sectarianism. Iran was increasingly emphasizing the importance of pan-Islamism. This policy seemed to be aimed at Saudi Arabia and the pan-Islamist Al-Qa'idah leaders such as Ayman al-Zawahiri, whose tape released in February stressed the importance of pan-Islamism by calling on Muslims to unite "even if they are Afghans, Persians, Turks or Kurds".[142]

The US was calling on European states to take firmer economic measures in response to Iran's nuclear policies.[143] In order to counter this, Khamenei sought to pressure Saudi Arabia, which Iranian officials saw as the linchpin of US regional strategy. The Iranians were particularly concerned about Saudi oil diplomacy[144] which they believed would lower the price of oil and deprive Iran of much needed revenues. At the same time, Khamenei allowed Ali Larijani to continue with the negotiating track, seeking to persuade Russia to join Iran in forming a gas cartel to contain Saudi influence over world energy markets. Khamenei's proposal was aimed at putting Iran at the centre of a geopolitical alliance against the US. His second objective seemed to be to offer Saudi Arabia a stark choice, change your oil and regional policies, or face joint Iranian-Russian pressure.

At his meeting with the Russian Security Council secretary Igor Ivanov, Khamenei said that Iran and Russia held "half of the world's gas reserves" and that "through mutual cooperation" they could form "an organization of gas exporting countries like OPEC".[145] He made it clear that he considered Iranian-Russian relations to be strategic and that the two countries had a common interest in containing US influence in the region.[146]

A number of Iranian politicians welcomed the gas-cartel proposal. A member of the National Security and Foreign Policy Committee of the Majlis, Hamid Reza Haji-Baba'i, said such a cartel could lead to the formation of a new "centre of power" which could "resist Western powers" and parry US "economic and political pressures".[147] There was speculation that President Putin would raise the issue during his visit to Qatar, the world's third largest gas producer after Russia and Iran.[148] Khamenei also authorized his personal foreign policy adviser and former foreign minister, Ali Akbar Velayati, to open a channel of communication with President Putin on the nuclear issue. The Velayati channel seemed to be aimed at strengthening Larijani's position without publicly offending President Ahmadinezhad. Indeed one Iranian MP, Javad Jahangirzadeh, who is a member of the National Security and Foreign Policy Committee of the Iranian Majlis, said that Larijani and Velayati "do not have contradictory positions on the nuclear issue".[149] This became clear during Velayati's visit to Moscow. Asked to comment on Moscow's support for UN resolutions passed against Iran, Velayati said that although Iran "was not happy with Moscow's move", one had also to consider that Russia had "succeeded in postponing [the adoption] of the anti-Iran resolution for one year".[150] Characterizing Putin's message to Iran as "a major strategic step" by Russia to expand its relations with Iran, Velayati declared: "Tehran-Moscow relations have strategic characteristics."[151]

Despite Iranian efforts to persuade Moscow to rely on Tehran as the linchpin of its regional strategy, President Putin was not disposed to put all his eggs in one basket. Thus during his visit to Saudi Arabia, Putin said that Moscow could consider providing assistance to Saudi Arabia to set up its own nuclear programme.

Putin expressed the hope that Russia would strengthen its ties with Muslim countries.[152]

By mid-February, President Ahmadinezhad's mismanagement of the Iranian economy, his pursuit of radical policies and his attempts to crack down on opposition to his government led to the formation of a coalition against Khamenei. Khamenei's intervention might have contained Ahmadinezhad's influence and limited his policy role, but it did not resolve any of Iran's major strategic problems. Although an internal EU study concluded that Iran might not be prevented from getting enough fissile material for a nuclear bomb[153], it was becoming increasingly clear that a nuclear Iran would be opposed by a de facto alliance of Israel, Egypt, Jordan and GCC states. Moreover, President Putin was exploiting Iran's so-called "strategic relationship" with Russia to improve the position of his own country in the Persian Gulf and the Middle East.

North Korea, with which Iran was trying to establish a "strategic relationship" and which was reportedly assisting Iran with its nuclear programme[154] was also acting in ways which could undermine the long-term viability of the Ahmadinezhad strategy. The North Korean nuclear agreement seems to have emboldened the Iranian proponents of negotiating along similar lines. Paradoxically, some Iranian hard-liners concluded that the North Korean model could be exploited to further their policy interests. They reportedly wanted to toughen Iran's demands in the expectation that the US would eventually agree to meet them.[155]

The conflict between Khamenei and Ahmadinezhad was not resolved through the issuance of statements on who formulated policy and who implemented it. In early February, Ahmadinezhad declared that Iran would not consider the option of suspending uranium enrichment. He said that Iran had "already stabilized its nuclear rights" and that "the Iranian nation" would hear the "good news" over the course of the next two months.[156]

However, Khamenei's adviser on international affairs, Ali Akbar Velayati did not rule out the possibility of suspending enrichment.[157] One indication of the conflict between Larijani and Ahmadinezhad was Larijani's statement at the Munich Security Conference that Iran did not intend to produce nuclear weapons and that it did not pose a threat to Israel. "How can atomic bombs solve the problems between Palestine and Israel? If an atomic bomb is dropped on Israel, all Muslims will die".[158] By mid-February, the Iranian Foreign Ministry was making contradictory statements as to whether Iran would be prepared to consider the possibility of suspending uranium enrichment.[159] Larijani proposed the establishment of "joint international uranium enrichment facilities" to assuage European concerns.[160] Such contradictory statements were indicative of the tug-of-war over nuclear policy, as well as of increasing factionalism at the highest echelons of the Iranian state.

Conclusion

The vacillation in Iranian policy was undoubtedly indicative of a major dispute at the highest echelons of the Iranian leadership. Khamenei's inability to resolve the issue and his refusal to bring the issue to a head indicates that he does not believe that he is politically strong enough to confront any of the protagonists without damaging his own domestic position. He needs Ahmadinezhad to increase the pressure on the US and Israel throughout the region. He also needs Larijani to take advantage of the instability generated by Ahmadinezhad to further the country's interests in the foreign policy arena. However, Ahmadinezhad and Larijani are pursuing vastly different strategies and the disarray in the Iranian leadership has also led to the formation of a broad alliance against Khamenei. So far he has been unable to separate the issue of his leadership from the dispute over the choice of strategy. It is unlikely that he will succeed in doing so in the near or medium term.

However, the dispute over the choice of strategy in Tehran is increasingly spilling over into other countries. The de facto collaboration between Israel and Saudi Arabia and other Sunni-majority Arab states might embolden Al-Qa'idah's pan-Islamist leaders such as Ayman al-Zawahiri. It is too early to say whether this will lead Ahmadinezhad's radical allies to seek a modus vivendi with pan-Islamist Sunni and Salafi radicals to challenge the fledgling Sunni alliance against Iran under the pretext of containing the influence of "Zionism" in the region.

In the geostrategic environment of late 2006-early 2007 the Iranian president seemed to be operating on the assumption that a combination of asymmetric threats and Iran's nuclear capability are sufficient to give it some kind of existential deterrent. However neither Rafsanjani nor the "reformists" believe that the risks associated with the Ahmadinezhad strategy are acceptable.

The grand coalition against the Iranian president was designed to compel Ayatollah Khamenei to change his domestic political and regional strategies. Khamenei has been moving tentatively in the direction of accommodating the president's opponents while supporting a multi-pronged offensive against US interests in the Middle East, Latin America and the Far East. However, Khamenei is also acutely aware of the vulnerability of his own position. Although Khamenei is on the same side as Ahmadinezhad from an ideological point of view, his behaviour suggests that in the assessment of the risks associated with the Ahmadinezhad strategy he is closer to Larijani. Clearly Khamenei believes that his power base with the Ahmadinezhad coalition is not broad enough to govern the country effectively.

Ahmadinezhad has responded to his coalition's defeat in the recent elections by seeking to cause foreign policy provocations that will lock his opponents into supporting radical policies. The alternative would be to try to work with other conservative groups to resolve the dispute over the choice of strategy. However, that will probably lead to the marginalization of his group because it lacks support in economic institutions and the clerical establishment. As long as the president lacks support in such key institutions he will find it difficult to dominate the state apparatus despite the support he enjoys in the intelligence and interior ministries and the Islamic Revolution Guards Corps.

As far as the nuclear issue is concerned, the dispute is likely to remain the potential size of Iran's nuclear arsenal, as well as the range and number of its delivery systems. Thus barring a major crisis in the near term, the dispute is likely to be between different advocates of nuclear opacity. Ahmadinezhad and his supporters, however, have a limited amount of time to settle the dispute in their favour. The president's declining popularity and the failure of his economic policies will not endear him to Iran's young population in the long run. The increasing political pressure on Khamenei will not make it easy for the supreme leader to support the president, whose opponents are just as determined to take advantage of Ahmadinezhad's radicalism to reduce Khamenei to a figurehead.

It is unlikely that Mesbah-Yazdi and Ahmadinezhad will be able to muzzle the clerical establishment for too long. Their best hope is to declare a state of emergency in the event of a major crisis involving the US and the EU and Israel and to use the concept of Mahdism to galvanize support among those who are prepared to sacrifice their lives for the regime. In the Iranian system the supreme jurisconsult Khamene'i is the Mahdi's deputy, and this has been recognized by the clerical establishment. However, a more concerted effort to justify rule by decree is likely to run up against significant political opposition inside and outside the clerical establishment and theological seminaries. Indeed, Mesbah-Yazdi and his supporters, such as Gharavian, recognized this and moderated their tone somewhat. In the event of a major international crisis Mesbah-Yazdi will seek to muzzle the opponents of the regime. However, if a prolonged crisis leads to the imposition of tougher sanctions and if there is no political progress, then he, and possibly Khamene'i himself, are likely to face serious challenges to their power.

Endnotes

[1] See IRNA, 2 September 2002, BBC Monitoring, see also Ray Takeyh, *Hidden Iran: Paradox and Power in the Islamic Republic* (New York: Times Books, 2006, p35.

[2] For a succinct account of the realignment of forces in Iranian politics see Ali Gheissari and Vali Nasr, *Democracy in Iran: History and the Quest for Liberty* (Oxford and New York: Oxford university Press, 2006), p151-8.

[3] See Hamed Irani, "Qom Concerned Over New Intelligence Appointments," Roozonline, November 2, 2005, Golnaz Esfandiari, "Iran: Qom Authorities Crack Down on Sufis", Radio Free Europe/Radio Liberty, February 16, 2006, Vahid Sepehri, "Rift Emerging Between President and Clerics", *Radio Free Europe/Radio Liberty*, January 30, 2007.

[4] See Amir Taheri, "Iran: The Other Clock Is Ticking", *Asharq al-Awsat*, February 10, 2006. See also Bill Samii, "Iran: Resurgence of Religio-Political Society Raises Concerns", R*adio Free Europe/Radio Liberty*, July 11, 2006.

[5] Ibid. On Hojjatieh during this period see David Menashri, *Iran: A Decade of War and Revolution* (New York: Homes and Meier Publishers, 1990), Nikola B. Schahgaldian: *The Clerical Establishment in Iran* (Santa Monica, Rand Corporation, 1989).

[6] See Bill Samii, "Iran: Resurgence of Religio-Political Society Raises Concerns", R*adio Free Europe/Radio Liberty*, July 11, 2006, Bill Samii, "Iran: Early Race For Clerical Assembly Gets Bitter", *Radio Free Europe/Radio Liberty*, September 22, 2006.

[7] See Bill Samii, "Iran: Resurgence of Religio-Political Society Raises Concerns", R*adio Free Europe/Radio Liberty*, July 11, 2006, Bill Samii, "Iran: Early Race For Clerical Assembly Gets Bitter", *Radio Free Europe/Radio Liberty*, September 22, 2006.

[8] See Bill Samii, "Iran: Early Race For Clerical Assembly Gets Bitter", *Radio Free Europe/Radio Liberty*, September 22, 2006.

[9] *Fars News Agency*, 19 August 2005, see also Bill Samii, "Iran: Resurgence of Religio-Political Society Raises Concerns", R*adio Free Europe/Radio Liberty*, July 11, 2006.

[10] See Bill Samii, "Iran: Resurgence of Religio-Political Society Raises Concerns", *Radio Free Europe/Radio Liberty*, July 11, 2006.

[11] Ibid.

[12] See for example, Amir Taheri, "Iran: The Other Clock Is Ticking", *Asharq al-Awsat*, February 10, 2006, Alan Peters, "Iran's 'Let's Roll' Beginning?", *Regime Change Iran*, January 7, 2006, Kenneth R. Timmerman, "Iran's Nuclear Zealot", *Project Syndicate*, January 11, 2006, Kenneth R. Timmerman, "Iranian President Sees End of World Order", *NewMax.com*, January 24, 2006.

[13] See for example, Amir Taheri, "Iran: The Other Clock Is Ticking", *Asharq al-Awsat*, February 10, 2006.

[14] See Wilfried Buchta, *Who Rules Iran: The Structure of Power in the Islamic Republic* (Washington: Washington Institute for Near East Policy, 2000), pp. 162, 168.

[15] See Babak Ganji, *President Mahmud Ahmadinezhad: Turning Point in Iranian Politics and Strategy?*, Conflict Studies Research Centre, October 2005.

[16] On this point see Babak Ganji, *Iran and Israel: Asymmetric Warfare and Regional Strategy*, Conflict Studies Research Centre, October 2006.

[17] See for example, Amir Taheri, "Iran: The Other Clock Is Ticking", *Asharq al-Awsat*, February 10, 2006.

[18] See Shahram Rafizadeh, "Iranian Cleric Okays use of Nuclear Weapons", *Roozonline*, 14 February 2006, BBC Monitoring.

[19] See Shahram Rafizadeh, "Iranian Cleric Okays Use of Nuclear Weapons!", Roozonline, 14 February 2006, BBC Monitoring. See also Patrick Clawson and Michael Rubin, *Eternal Iran: Continuity and Chaos.* (Basingstoke and New York: Palgrave Macmillan, 2005), pp. 139-144. They do not say anything about Khamenei's role but provide a short account of Iranian activities and views of Iranian leaders.

[20] See Shahram Rafizadeh, "Iranian Cleric Okays Use of Nuclear Weapons!", Roozonline, 14 February 2006, BBC Monitoring.

[21] See *Iranian Students News Agency*, 18 February 2006.

[22] Shahram Rafizadeh, "Iranian Clerics Okays Use of Nuclear Weapons!", Roozonline, 14 February 2006, BBC Monitoring.

[23] See the report on Armin's comments at http://www.bazbaran.ir.

[24] Ibid.

[25] On Hajjarian's activities see Ali M. Ansari, *Iran, Islam and Democracy: The Politics of Managing Change* (London, Chatham House, 2006), pp 219-22. On the assassination attempt against Hajjarian see, Geneive Abdo, "Khatami Ally Is Shot and Wounded in Tehran Attack", *International Herald Tribune*, March 13, 2000. On the realignment of forces during the 2005 presidential elections see Babak Ganji, *President Mahmud Ahmadinezhad: Turning Point in Iranian Politics and Strategy?*, Conflict Studies Research Centre, October 2005.

[26] See the daily, *Hemayat*, 30 April 2006. See also Bill Samii, "Iran: Resurgence of Religio-Political Society Raises Concerns", *Radio Free Europe/Radio Liberty*, July 11, 2006.

[27] Bill Samii, "Iran: Resurgence of Religio-Political Society Raises Concerns", *Radio Free Europe/Radio Liberty*, July 11, 2006. See Abdolkarim Sorush's interview with *Roozonline*, 30 January 2006.

[28] See Abdolkarim Sorush's interview with *Roozonline*, 30 January 2006.

[29] For a detailed report see http://fardanews.com, 7 March 2006.

[30] Ibid.

[31] Ibid.

[32] On this point see Gareth Smyth, *Fundamentalists, Pragmatists, and the Rights of the Nation: Iranian Politics and Nuclear Confrontation*, (Washington D.C.: The Century Foundation, 2006).

[33] "Iran 'could share nuclear skills'", BBC News, Middle East, http://news.bbc.co.uk, 25 April 2006.

[34] See "Report: Japan Eyeing Sanctions Against Iran in Nuclear Weapons Dispute", *Fox News*, June 4, 2006, "Japan to support sanctions against Iran", *Financial Times*, June 23, 2006.

[35] On this point see *Islamic Republic of Iran News Network*, (IRINN), 4 June 2006, BBC Monitoring.

[36] For a good account of the differing perspectives on the role of the Foreign Policy Council see Bill Samii, "Iran: New Foreign Policy Council Could Curtail Ahmadinejad's Power", *Radio Free Europe/Radio Liberty*, June 29, 2006.

[37] See Bill Samii, "Iran: Resurgence of Religio-Political Society Raises Concerns", *Radio Free Europe/Radio Liberty*, July 11, 2006.

[38] For the text of the directive see *Iranian Students News Agency*, 3 July 2006. For Khamenei's role in factional balancing see International Crisis Group, *Iran: Ahmadi-Nejad's Tumultuous Presidency*, Middle East Briefing N.21, Tehran/Brussels, 6 February 2007, p. 19.

[39] On this point see, Babak Ganji, *Iran and Israel: Asymmetric Warfare and Regional Strategy*, Conflict Studies Research Centre, 27 October 2006.

[40] For a good account of the differing perspectives on the role of the Foreign Policy Council see Bill Samii, "Iran: New Foreign Policy Council Could Curtail Ahmadinejad's Power", *Radio Free Europe/Radio Liberty*, June 29, 2006.

[41] See "President inaugurates Arak heavy water plant", *Islamic Republic News Agency*, August 26, 2006, "Ahmadinejad: Iran not a threat to any state", *Islamic Republic News Agency*, August 26, 2006, "Defiant Iran unveils heavy-water plant", *Jerusalem Post*, August 26, 2006, Ali Akbar Dareini, "Iran Opens Heavy-Water Nuclear Plant", The Associated Press, August 26, 2006.

[42] On this point see Babak Ganji, *Iran and Israel: Asymmetric Warfare and Regional Strategy*, Conflict Studies Research Centre, Middle East Series 06/49, October 2006.

[43] For Bahonar's remarks see: *Sharif News*, August 25, 2006, at http://sharifnews.com/. See also "Iranian Statements on the Occasion of the Inauguration of the Arak Heavy Water Plant, *Middle East Media Research Institute* (MEMRI), Special Dispatch Series, No.1271, August 30, 2006.

[44] Babak Ganji, *Iran and Israel: Asymmetric Warfare and Regional Strategy*, Conflict Studies Research Centre, Middle East Series, October 2006.

[45] See "Khatami labels US policy 'a joke'", *BBC News, Middle East,* http://news.bbc.co.uk, 2 November 2006.

[46] See "Japan to support sanctions against Iran", *Financial Times*, June 23, 2006, "Japan braces to lose part of Iranian oil mega-project", *Agence France Press*, October 6, 2006; "Iran's Azadegan Cancellation A Blow to Japanese Energy Strategy, Says FACTS". *Middle East Economic Survey*, 18 December 2006.

[47] See "U.S. Approves $458 Million Sale of SM-3 Interceptors to Japan", *Defense Security Cooperation Agency News Release*, June 7, 2006, Joseph Coleman, "U.S., Japan Expand Missile-Defense Plan", *The Associated Press*, June 23, 2006, "Japan Wants Missile Defense 'As Soon As Possible': Defense Chief, *Agence France Press*, 6 July 2006, "Japan Considers Preemptive Strike Against North Korea", *The Associated Press*, July 10, 2006, "Yomiuri Shimbun: New Threat Calls for New Defense Initiative", October 11, 2006, at http://www.missilethreat.com/, Japan Tests New SAM in Texas, with Anti-Cruise Missile Capability, December 1, 2006, U.S. and Japan Plan New SM-3 Maintenance Base, *United Press International,* December 6, 2006.

[48] See Simon Henderson, *Naval Exercises Off Bahrain: Preventing Proliferation between North Korea and Iran*, Policy Watch # 1157, The Washington Institute for Near East Policy, October 27, 2006.

[49] For a detailed account of Rafsanjani's views on the guardianship of the supreme jurisconsult and the role of the Assembly of Experts see: "Iran press: Interview with Rafsanjani on Assembly of Experts, selecting leader", *Iran Press Review from BBC Monitoring*, 1 August 2006, BBC Monitoring.

[50] Ibid.

[51] See the coverage of Rafsanjani's activities by the strongly pro-Ahmadinezhad Ansar News at www.ansarnews.com.

[52] *Partowe Sokhan*, 23 August 2007.

[53] See "Iran: Text of Khomeyni's letter on agreeing to cease-fire after eight-year war", *Iranian Labour News Agency*, 29 September 2006, BBC Monitoring. See also "Iran former IRGC chief wrote at Rafsanjani's behest – MP", *Baztab*, web site, 30 September 2006, BBC Monitoring, "Iran: Former IRGC commander on discussions with Khomeyni over ending war", *Baztab*, web site, 28 September 2006, BBC Monitoring.

[54] See for example Iranian Labour News Agency's interview with Hoseyn Mar'ashi, *Iranian Labour News Agency*, 1 October 2006.

[55] See also "Iran former IRGC chief wrote at Rafsanjani's behest – MP", *Baztab*, web site, 30 September 2006, BBC Monitoring, "Iran: Former IRGC commander on discussions with Khomeyni over ending war", *Baztab*, web site, 28 September 2006, BBC Monitoring.

[56] *Kayhan*, 3 October 2007.

[57] See for example *Kayhan* 1 October 2006, See also *Iranian press menu on 1 October 2006*, BBC Monitoring.

[58] See for example Iranian Labour News Agency's interview with Hoseyn Mar'ashi, *Iranian Labour News Agency*, 1 October 2006.

[59] See Ziba Mir-Hosseini and Richard Tapper, *Islam and Democracy in Iran: Eshkevari and the Quest for Reform* (London: I.B. Tauris, 2006).

[60] On this point see Amir Taheri, "Schism in Iran", *New York Post*, October 22, 2006.

[61] Ibid.

[62] See Golnaz Esfandiari, "Iran: Outspoken Ayatollah Alleges Official Persecution", *Radio Free Europe/Radio Liberty*, October 6, 2006.

[63] Ibid.

[64] Ibid.

[65] Ibid.

[66] Ibid.

[67] Amir Taheri, "Schism in Iran", *New York Post*, October 22, 2006.

[68] See Bill Samii, "Iran: Battles Begin As Assembly Candidates Await Vetting", *Radio Free Europe/Radio Liberty*, October 12, 2006.

[69] See "Hashemi-Samareh replaces Jannati as deputy interior minister", *Mehr News Agency*, September 27, 2006.

[70] See International Crisis Group, *Iran: Ahmadi-Nejad's Tumultuous Presidency*, Middle East Briefing N.21, Tehran/Brussels, 6 February 2007.

[71] See for example the article by Mehrdad Sheybani, *Roozonline*, at http://roozonline.com, October 13, 2006.

[72] Ibid.

[73] See *Iranian Students News Agency*, 1 October 2006.

[74] For a good article on the political manoeuvres during this period see Omid Me'marian, "Khamenei supports Ahmadinejad", Roozonline, at http://roozonline.com, 22 November 2006.

[75] See *Farda News*, 10 October 2006.

[76] Ibid.

[77] Ibid.

[78] Ibid.

[79] See Mehdi Khalaji, *The Significance of Iran's December Elections*, Policy Watch #1173, The Washington Institute for Near East Policy, December 11, 2006.

[80] See *Fars News Agency* 11 December, 2006.

[81] See Ahmadinezhad's weblog reproduced by *Gooya News* at http://news.gooya.eu, 13 December 2006.

[82] See *Gooya News* at http://news.gooya.eu, 12 December 2006.

[83] For the text of the letter see *Gooya News* at http://news.gooya.eu, 14 December 2006.

[84] See the report by *Gooya News* at http://news.gooya.eu, 12 December 2006.

[85] See *Gooya News* at http://news.gooya.eu, 12 December 2006.

[86] See *Iranian Labour News Agency*, 12 December 2006.

[87] For an account of the conflict between various radical and conservative factions see Bill Samii, "Rivalries Heat Up Among Iran's Conservatives", *Radio Free Europe/Radio Liberty*, April 25, 2006. On Naderan's ties to the Revolutionary Guards see: "Iran's New President Glorifies Martyrdom", *Middle East Media Research Institute* (MEMRI), Special Dispatch Series - No. 945, July 29, 2005.

[88] For a detailed account of the debate see *Iranian Labour News Agency*, 3 December 2006.

[89] See International Crisis Group, *Iran: Ahmadi-Nejad's Tumultuous Presidency*, Middle East Briefing N.21, Tehran/Brussels, 6 February 2007, p. 19, fn. 46.

[90] See Carl Mortished, "Iran turns from dollar to euro in oil sales", *The Times*, December 22, 2006. See also: Toni Straka, "Killing the dollar in Iran", *Asia Times*, August 26, 2005, "Will Iran's oil kill the dollar?", *Aljazeera.com*, September 14, 2005, also "The new threat facing the dollar", *Money Week*, 21 March 2006, Milton Ezrati, "Iran's plan to weaken the dollar will fail", *The Christian Science Monitor*, March 29, 2006. For US-Chinese negotiations see: "Paulson, Bernanke to lead top US team to Beijing", *Agence France Press*, 28 November 2006, Carin Zissis, "Facing China's 'Peaceful Rise'", *Council on Foreign Relations*, December 5, 2006, Carin Zissis, "On Trade, A Superpower Summit", *Council on Foreign Relations*, December 15, 2006.

[91] See Mel Levine, Alex Turkeltaub and Alex Gorbansky, "3 Myths About the Iran Conflict", *Washington Post*, 8 February 2006.

[92] For a good article see Scott Johnson and Michael Hastings, "Oil exports were supposed to pay for the reconstruction. Instead, they've been stifled.", *Newsweek*, January 30, 2006.

[93] See "Oil slips on Saudi supply offer, Iran supports", *Iran Mania*, January 24 2006.

[94] Ibid.

[95] See "Iran expected to raise spectre of oil weapon", *Iran Mania*, January 27 2006.

[96] Ibid. On the Iran oil study see Roger Stern, "The Iranian petroleum crisis and United States national security", *Proceedings of the National Academy of Sciences of the United States of America*, January 2, 2007, Roger Stern, "Iran actually is short of oil", *International Herald Tribune*, January 8, 2007, "Iran: U.S. Expert Predicts Oil-Export Crisis Within A Decade, *Radio Free Europe/Radio Liberty*, January 12, 2007.

[97] See Roger Stern, "The Iranian petroleum crisis and United States national security", *Proceedings of the National Academy of Sciences of the United States of America*, January 2, 2007, Roger Stern, "Iran actually is short of oil", *International Herald Tribune*, January 8,

2007, "Iran: U.S. Expert Predicts Oil-Export Crisis Within A Decade, *Radio Free Europe/Radio Liberty*, January 12, 2007.

[98] See "Al-Hayat editor: Iran is Trying to Position Itself as 'The Only Power in the Region'", *Al-Hayat*, 13 December 2006, *Middle East Media Research Institute* (MEMRI), Special Dispatch Series – No. 1398, December 19, 2006.

[99] See "Saudi king says Iran putting region in danger: paper", *Reuters*, 27 January 2007.

[100] See Daniel Byman, "Saudi Arabia's own Iraq nightmare", *salon.com*, February 8, 2007.

[101] See "40 institutes boycott Iran think tank over Holocaust conference", *The Associated Press*, December 17, 2006.

[102] See for example an editorial by *Baztab*, 19 December 2006.

[103] See Nazila Fathi "Tehran Radio Lets Critics Vent Over Iran's Nuclear Plans", *The New York Times*, December 31 2006.

[104] "Former Iran leaders speak out against nuclear policy", 30 December 2006 at http://news.yahoo.

[105] Ibid.

[106] See Iran says UNSC resolution 'stillborn', more resolutions will not work", *Islamic Republic of Iran News Network*, 21 January 2007, BBC Monitoring.

[107] See "Iran president says 'enemies' powerless in face of Iranian nation", *Islamic Republic of Iran News Network*, 21 January 2007, BBC Monitoring, "President presents budget bill, says will not retreat in nuclear case", *Iranian TV*, 21 January 2006, BBC Monitoring.

[108] See *Iranian Students News Agency*, 21 January 2007.

[109] See "Attack on Iran would jeopardize international flow of oil – Majlis deputies", *Mehr News Agency*, 20 January 2006, BBC Monitoring.

[110] *Kayhan*, 22 January 2007, see also Iran press: Editorial says threat of us military attack psychological warfare, *Kayhan*, 22 January 2007, BBC Monitoring, Amir Taheri, "The Return of Saddam Hussein", *Asharq Alawsat*, January 26, 2007, and "The Middle East on a Collision Course (5): Iran Steps up Threats to Retaliate in the Event of an American Attack", *Middle East Media Research Institute* (MEMRI), Special Dispatch Series – No. 1457, February 9, 2007.

[111] *Kayhan*, 22 January 2007, see also Amir Taheri, "The Return of Saddam Hussein", *Asharq Alawsat*, January 26, 2007, and "The Middle East on a Collision Course (5): Iran Steps up Threats to Retaliate in the Event of an American Attack", *Middle East Media Research Institute* (MEMRI), Special Dispatch Series – No. 1457, February 9, 2007.

[112] See *Kayhan*, 28 January, 2007. See also "Editor of Iranian Kayhan Daily Reacts to U.N. Resolution Against Holocaust Denial: 'The Resolution Prepares the UN's Corpse for Burial in the Graveyard of History", *Middle Media Research Institute* (MEMRI), Special Dispatch Series –No.1443, January 30, 2007. See also Nikola Krastev, "World: Holocaust Denial Draws Intense Criticism", *Radio Free Europe/Radio Liberty*, January 30, 2007.

[113] See *Kayhan*, 28 January, 2007. See also "Editor of Iranian Kayhan Daily Reacts to U.N. Resolution Against Holocaust Denial: 'The Resolution Prepares the UN's Corpse for Burial in the Graveyard of History", *Middle Media Research Institute* (MEMRI), Special Dispatch Series –No.1443, January 30, 2007.

[114] *Kayhan*, 5 February 2007. See also "The Middle East on a Collision Course (5): Iran Steps up Threats to Retaliate in the Event of an American Attack", *Middle East Media Research Institute* (MEMRI), Special Dispatch Series – No. 1457, February 9, 2007.

[115] See the report "Defence Minister: Military action against Iran is tantamount to suicide", *Iran*, 4 February 2007, BBC Monitoring.

[116] Ibid. See also "The Middle East on a Collision Course (5): Iran Steps up Threats to Retaliate in the Event of an American Attack", *Middle East Media Research Institute* (MEMRI), Special Dispatch Series – No. 1457, February 9, 2007.

[117] See Mohammad Ali Ramin's interview with Roozonline at http://www.roozonline.com.

[118] See Mohammad Ali Ramin's interview with *Baztab* web site, 28 December 2006. See also "Mohammad Ali Ramin, Advisor to Iranian President Ahmadinejad: 'Hitler Was Jewish'", January 3, 2007, *Middle East Media Research Institute* (MEMRI), Special Dispatch Series – No. 1408, January 3, 2007.

[119] See Mohammad Ali Ramin's interview with *Baztab* web site, 28 December 2006. See also "Mohammad Ali Ramin, Advisor to Iranian President Ahmadinejad: 'Hitler Was Jewish'", January 3, 2007, *Middle East Media Research Institute* (MEMRI), Special Dispatch Series – No. 1408, January 3, 2007.

[120] See "Revealed: Israel plans nuclear strike on Iran", *The Sunday Times*, 7 January 2007.

---

[121] See "Israel rejects report it may attack Iran's nuclear program - with nuclear weapons", *International Herald Tribune*, January 7, 2007.

[122] See "Iran Warns Attacker 'Would Quickly Regret' Entering Its Territory', *All Headlines News*, January 7, 2007.

[123] See "Larijani: Iran to continue cooperation with IAEA based on NPT", *Islamic Republic News Agency*, February 14, 2007.

[124] For Mottaki's comments see "Iran to celebrate becoming a nuclear country", *Iranian Students News Agency*, December 26, 2006.

[125] See "Larijani: Atomic talks can continue if Iran is recognized as a nuclear country", *Islamic Republic News Agency*, February 14, 2007.

[126] *Islamic Republic News Agency*, 8 January 2007, *Iranian Students News Agency*, 8 January 2007.

[127] See *Jomhuri-ye Eslami*, 9 January 2007. See also "Iranian Domestic Criticism of Iran's Nuclear Strategy", *Middle East Media Research Institute* (MEMRI), Inquiry and Analysis Series – No. 317, January 24, 2007.

[128] Ibid.

[129] Ibid.

[130] Ibid.

[131] See for example a *Jomhuri-ye Eslami* article by Hasan Sobhani, 21 January 2007. See also "Iranian press menu on January 21 2007", BBC Monitoring.

[132] See Lionel Beehar, "Presidential Skeptics in Iran", *Council on Foreign Relations*, January 23, 2007.

[133] See Vahid Sepehri, "Rift Emerging Between President and Clerics", *Radio Free Europe/Radio Liberty*, January 30, 2007.

[134] "Ahmadinejad defiant on nuke program", *The Associated Press*, February 1 2007.

[135] See "Iran and Venezuela back oil cuts", 14 January 2007, BBC News Americas, http://news.bbc.co.uk Natalie Obiko Pearson, "Iran and Venezuela plan anti-U.S. fund", *The Associated Press*, 14 January 2007, "Iran and Venezuela agree on $2-billion anti-U.S. fund", *Aljazeera.com*, 14 January 2007.

[136] See Jeffrey Donovan, "U.S.: Bush Moves to Contain Iranian Influence", *Radio Free Europe/Radio Liberty*, January 18, 2007. See also "Iran to contribute to Iraq's security - intelligence minister", *Iranian radio*, 14 January 2007, BBC Monitoring, and "Iran-Iraq discuss mutual security issues", *Iranian Students News Agency*, 15 January 2007, BBC Monitoring.

[137] See Jeffrey Donovan, "U.S.: Bush Moves to Contain Iranian Influence", *Radio Free Europe/Radio Liberty*, January 18, 2007.

[138] See "No question of halt in Iran's Larijani-Solana 11-article agreement: Informed source", *Islamic Republic News Agency*, 17 January, 2007.

[139] See "Iran denies report on Saudi mediation between Tehran and Washington", *Islamic Republic News Agency*, January 15, 2007, and "Saudi says not mediating between Iran and US", *Agence France Press*, 16 January 2007.

[140] See for example Ahmed al-Jarallah, " US military strike on Iran seen by April 07", *Arab Times*, 14 January 2007.

[141] See "Mottaki: London should account for what it has done to Iran since 1979", *Islamic Republic News Agency*, February 13, 2007.

[142] See "Al-Qaeda's No.2 calls for Muslim unity", *The Associated Press*, 13 February 2007.

[143] See US urges Europe to boost Iran sanctions", *The Financial Times*, February 7, 2007 and "Differences over how to punish Iran's nuclear defiance strain international alliance", *Boston Herald*, February 8, 2007.

[144] See for example Nimrod Raphaeli, "The Middle East on a Collision Course (5): The Saudi Oil Weapon", *Middle East Media Research Institute* (MEMRI), Inquiry and Analysis Series, No. 326, February 14, 2007.

[145] See "Supreme Leader stresses importance of Iran-Russia cooperation", *Islamic Republic News Agency*, January 28, 2007, see also "Energy Jihad", *Kommersant*, January 30, 2007.

[146] See "Supreme Leader stresses importance of Iran-Russia cooperation", *Islamic Republic News Agency*, January 28, 2007.

[147] See Iranian Politicians Support Gas-Cartel Proposal", *Radio Free Europe/Radio Liberty*, February 7, 2007.

[148] See "Putin may discuss OPEC for gas cartel during visit to Persian Gulf", *The Associated Press*, February 6, 2007.

[149] On this point see Vahid Sepehri, "Iran: Velayati's Moscow Visit Seen As Strengthening Relations With Russia", *Radio Free Europe/Radio Liberty*, February 13 2007.

[150] See "Velayati: Moscow to use its influence to prevent another anti-Iran resolution", *Islamic Republic News Agency*, 11 February 2007.

[151] See "Ahmadinejad's response to Putin's message, strategic: Velayati", *Islamic Republic News Agency*, February 11, 2007.

[152] See "Russia could help Saudi in atomic energy-Putin", *Reuters*, February 12, 2007. See also Brian Whitmore, "Russia: Putin To Take His Message To The Persian Gulf", *Radio Free Europe/Radio Liberty*, February 9, 2007.

[153] See Daniel Dombey, "EU report on Iran: Details and full text", *The Financial Times*, February 13, 2007.

[154] See for example Con Coughlin, "The ominous relationship between North Korea and Iran", *Daily Telegraph*, 24 January 2007.

[155] "Iran eyeing North Korean model", *Los Angeles Times*, February 14, 2007, "Iran may follow in North Korea's footsteps", *The Sydney Morning Herald*, 16 February 2007. See also Paul Hughes, "North Korea deal shows the way on Iran – ElBaradei", *Reuters India*, February 16, 2007.

[156] See "Ahmadinejad to give good news to Iranians", *Fars News Agency*, 11 February 2007.

[157] *Reuters*, 15 February 2007.

[158] See "Larijani: Iran pledges not to produce nuclear weapons", *Islamic Republic News Agency*, February 13, 2007.

[159] See two contradictory statements by Iranian Foreign Ministry spokesman Mohammad Ali Hoseyni, "Enrichment suspension negotiable", *Islamic Republic News Agency*, February 12, 2007, "FM spokesman rules out suspension of uranium enrichment", *Islamic Republic News Agency*, 13 February 2007.

[160] *Islamic Republic News Agency*, 15 February 2007.

The author wishes to thank the Advanced Research and Assessment Group at the Defence Academy of the United Kingdom and BBC Monitoring for supporting this project.

Want to Know More ...?

See:

International Crisis Group, Iran: Ahmadi-Nejad's Tumultuous Presidency, Middle East Briefing N.21, Tehran/Brussels, 6 February 2007.

Ali M. Ansari, Iran, Islam and Democracy: The Politics of Managing Change (London, Chatham House, 2006)

Wilfried Buchta, Who Rules Iran?: The Structure of Power in the Islamic Republic (Washington D.C.: The Washington Institute for Near East Policy, 2000)

Ali Gheissari and Vali Nasr, Democracy in Iran: History and the Quest for Liberty (Oxford and New York: Oxford university Press, 2006)

Ziba Mir-Hosseini and Richard Tapper, Islam and Democracy in Iran: Eshkevari and the Quest for Reform (London: I.B. Tauris, 2006)

Ray Takeyh, Hidden Iran: Paradox and Power in the Islamic Republic (New York: Times Books, 2006)

<u>Disclaimer</u>

ISBN 978-1-905962-05-1